The Book of Z

Z

Also by
Rahat Kurd

The City That Is Leaving Forever: Kashmiri Letters
(with Sumayya Syed)

Cosmophilia

published by Talonbooks

The Book of Z

A Poem

Rahat Kurd

Talonbooks

Talonbooks
9259 Shaughnessy Street, Vancouver, British Columbia, Canada V6P 6R4
talonbooks.com

Talonbooks is located on xʷməθkʷəy̓əm, Sḵwx̱wú7mesh, and səlilwətaɬ Lands.

First printing: 2025
Typeset in Arno
Printed and bound in Canada on 100% post-consumer recycled paper

Talonbooks acknowledges the financial support of the Canada Council for the Arts, the Government of Canada through the Canada Book Fund, and the Province of British Columbia through the British Columbia Arts Council and the Book Publishing Tax Credit.

Library and Archives Canada Cataloguing in Publication

Title: The book of Z : poems / Rahat Kurd.
Names: Kurd, Rahat, author.
Identifiers: Canadiana 20250184400 | ISBN 9781772016895 (softcover)
Subjects: LCGFT: Poetry.
Classification: LCC PS8621.U73 B66 2025 | DDC C811/.6—dc23

MY MOUTH WILL BE FILLED WITH GENIAL, HONEY-SWEET WORDS, AS I TELL OF YUSUF'S BEAUTY AND ZULAIKHA'S PASSION. GOD [HU]SELF CALLS IT "THE MOST BEAUTIFUL OF STORIES."

—HAKIM NURUDDIN ABDURRAHMAN JAMI

1 In the Subjunctive Mood for Love
3 Zulaykha, Protagonist
17 Dear Yusuf
33 Zulaykha Addresses the Patriarchs
41 Ghalib Praises My Dream of Yusuf
49 Zulaykha Surveys Her Art History
63 Zulaykha Considers Her Options
75 Zulaykha Alone
93 Ashura
103 Akhlaq
109 Inheritance
115 Zulaykha Is Floored by Emily Dickinson's Poem 1311
123 Emily Dickinson's Work Ethic
127 Introspective Ghazal

129 Shukrana
131 Art Works Referred to in "Zulaykha Surveys Her Art History"
133 Epigraph Sources

In the Subjunctive Mood for Love

For women let down by my assigned anticlimax
I'd leave signs at every saray
        Warning: poet bros

For men in thrall to saviour complex
I'd leave provocations:
        I was the original lover in exile
        I was first to tear my collar
        I contained that universe – yes
        my spine bore me up each of the hundred thousand times
        I committed the sin of denying what I felt

I'd pelt stones for their exaggerations
demand how they dared claim the sun as their takhallus

For the ones who leave their homes seeking Haqq, Rahman,
the Name that remains unknown
I'd wish them riches   the dry and stony path

For those who remain who remain who remain
awaiting a wordless reality that transcends all Names
my steadfast ones   I'd offer my very jugular

Zulaykha,
Protagonist

UNION WITH THE BELOVED, THOUGH ETERNAL, IS ALSO – WITHIN OUR WORLD OF SPACE AND TIME – EPHEMERAL. IT IS A VALID MANIFESTATION OF THE REAL (AL-HAQQ). BUT IT CANNOT BE POSSESSED.

—MICHAEL SELLS

The moment I see him is missed footing on a downward stair. The moment I see him is a premonition remembered too late. The first time I see him a faint alarm rises to deafen an inadequate grammar. Subject verb object will not convey how wildly space and time, having propelled our lives across billions of improbabilities towards this encounter, now stop short

The sublime workings of physics, geologic time, planets aligned at my birth leave me indifferent, but desire must have its way, push past unprepared reason, overwhelm the earthbound human body, force the contest between polite manners and mortality, demand comparisons to suns and oceans, strain the resources of poets and public treasuries and nuclear-disarmament collectives

It's a shock I'll never recover from, space, that dealer of swaggering enormities, that crutch of human consciousness, leaving so little of itself between our faces, knowing I will prove unequal to closing the remaining distance, no unscalable walls, no impassable mountain ranges, just this space folding itself meekly, space bowing humbly, before the tyrant of time

His face brings slow astonishment, wonder of desire, warmth to a sensibility chilled by perpetual winter. Mantle of solitude, marked for me from birth, promises finally to slide off my shoulders. Before the alarm begins to shrill. Before the drugging wonder becomes the calamity of separation, before the patriarchs overwrite my electrified embodiment, let me grasp by a micron the truer prize on which women need me not to lose my grip, the narrative charge of my first person. As if my own eyes called it into being. When I look at him my discernment saves the moment from oblivion. My desire makes possible our future in all its vexed and lyrical tellings

Yusuf washes dishes at my sink. Poetry might begin here, in the flow of water
over his fingers, in the rhythm of his arms, in the rise of his torso from hips
braced in the simple labour from which we both know he'll win freedom
soon enough. Cosseted as I am, sheltered with all my prestige, I know I dwell
in margins marked off by prerogatives of capital, social codes of men who
write his hours, brother schemers, despot dreamers

To look at him is to be nearly blinded with an apprehension of something worse than loss, the space between us impassive, while time, unfurling its banner, shakes all my future nights free of his radiance, trampling my chest with *never having* the very same instant desire springs to life within it –

Unreasoningly I feel my fury rise and turn to horses –

My fury requisitions all the horses that ever raced across poetry, from Chang'an to Ürümqi, from Samarkand to Smyrna, sweeping across all the cities that ever sang promises to women of enduring safety and love, betraying them, leaving them undefended –

I see them all vividly, the cities we will win and lose, how we will weep over their orphans and curse their pillagers, before time releases its vengeful grip on the sovereignty of my past and the nights of my future –

My best critics will advise my readers
with every eye that falls upon this line
Zulaykha sees Yusuf for the first time

And I envy the flow of water over Yusuf's fingers. To extract the feeling I want from him, to demand what no king or vizier, no sycophant would sanction, would make me a tyrant more petty than they, coveting, concocting an art and a science

to bring his mouth onto mine
to make it stop time – to make it stop time

Dear Yusuf

THOU ANGEL BRINGST WITH THEE
A HEAVEN LIKE MAHOMET'S PARADISE

—JOHN DONNE

Dear Yusuf,

As a girl I wished for a small space of my own. A perch above a vista; a safe enclosure. Jami says I was the daughter of a Maghribi king, but I lack royal inclinations: to gaze on meadows and mountain peaks and breathe, *mine, all mine*, to discern the glacial age in a sip of icy river water, to give my attendants the order, *prepare the next expedition*. So strange to think – I hesitate – in flight from me, you sought the safety of a prison cell. Jami says I even watched while you slept. It must be true – I can barely breathe for the thought of you there, held in your straitened nights. In my mouth the taste for possession gathers. I envy the poet who allowed desire to move his pen, likening his beloved's body to land – lush, hidden, awaiting discovery

I think I'll steal the metaphor

Dear Yusuf,

Your eyelid's sleepy curve undoes all court painters' stern disciplines, sworn allegiances. Your face on its hesitant cusp plunges me back into retrospect, by turns thrilled and gloomy. The earliest manuscripts illuminating my love for you – made so slowly and for so few – hidden away as if by jinn under the command of Solomon – screen our art histories against our future dispossessions. Your unreachable repose becomes my well-fitted coat, my daggerless sleeves embroidered, *solitude, solitude infinite*. You remain the marvellous series of cravings to which I can still be reduced, to feed you witty vignettes, watch you laugh, see you savour cold grapes my fingers would be helpless not to proffer from silver bowls. My longing for continuity's filled with civility's pinnacle, this dastarkhan, forget empyrean realms, give me a man who understands his mouth is a trust from heaven, made for me

Dear Yusuf,

Your panicked flight from me mirrors a hazard more women face than men. Painters obedient to our patriarchs keep tracing the line of my outlaw arm, turning their backs on the millennia-long conundrum, the obduracy of the script I flip.

Girls and women might feel my hunger and thirst as their own and never walk my way. For them my scandal's a moral caution, a lesson in subsistence, self-denial, self-burial. Told how desire suffuses the clear lines of my eyes and mouth, they might pull off composure's mask in a private moment, to feel its bloom on their own faces, the wistfulness of God's words –

I was a treasure, hidden, and I wanted to be known

but who wants to be Zulaykha in the world that made her notorious?

World of boys and men whom no law, no border obstructs from flaunting open desire or leering some lower craving, who sever desire from its source –

forgetting to praise the Maker for the face that inspires it
forgetting my remorse, my fidelity to a higher ideal

Dear Yusuf,

To arrive at knowledge that terrifies, one must live a long time. To find oneself used instead of loved is to arrive in a present ransacked and evacuated by the past, to finally hear the alarm that has been tuning one's nerves to its shrill frequency. Heart and mind yoked to lament, gaze forced backward, bereft state flooding the intimate recesses of consciousness

Other humans call them a *system* – signals of calm, steadiness, absorption, capacities one never guessed could give life reason, wholeness, flow, pulsing between the organs to which, all this time, my poets attributed only the most frantic of passions –

Will poetry ever be required reading for pharmaceutical researchers?

Pronouncing him *pain devil*, Anne Carson sees Heathcliff, Emily Brontë's creation, ransacked so ruthlessly, unable to recover from the plunge that follows exaltation – canonical, epistemic Heathcliff, his chronic loneliness the appalling cautionary point of the anglophilic curriculum – the way radiant conviction comes to seem delusional in the sense-dulling aftermath, as if such radiance is not to be borne, nor lived with, which is to say, not loved – only seized in the moment

You could read the novel, and the long poem that analyzes the novel, and still not be prepared for the precipice from which Jaun Elia hurls himself in every searing line of "Punishment," seeking no relief for the pain of knowing his existence inflicts pain, only naming its symmetrical exactions, the way Heathcliff swears he can forgive his murderer (Cathy) – but not hers (also Cathy)

Other artists quail before the block of marble or the sized canvas the way I feared I might fail its symmetrical exactions, the desire that unfroze my ransacked, evacuated nervous system, flooding pain with relief, commanding me to live, against every puritan proscription –

Live before you die

Dear Yusuf,

The thing adults don't say to children enough – that sex is a life force, strong in some, cool or sublimated in others, how it ebbs and flows, how all of it could be fine, *we could all be totally fine if*

No one solves the dilemma. The best of men lapse, looking at women through the clouded lens of their century's failed poetics. Women set their teeth, start axe-throwing leagues. I hover at the periphery with the other social recalcitrants while the body keeps its rhythms, reminding me what it was to wake in the grip of the fever I gave your name at 4 a.m. some white nights. I write you from an era of renouncers, refrainers, abstainers from any substance but the longing my irritating mystics still claim superior to the triumph of physical union. Getting out of the demented snarl of what signals love in the amygdalas of some unfortunate men continues to kill more unfortunate women. No one solves the dilemma. Amid the many dissolutions of mass culture sprout rhetorics of self-abnegation, tiny houses where the cooled self can sleep, the relief, the dignity, that follow the shutting of a door

Dear Yusuf,

I look at men, sometimes, in the daylight my years still bestow, filling my eyes with benediction, good reasons to stay alive, still

I look at men, I admit, carefully – looks neither freely nor easily given, negotiated with my hard-won recomposed self –

Slipping from restraints and proscriptions issued to devout girls by God's gatekeepers, I find belonging in the flow of wind and water, in the sere and level field of my own discernment

I look at their faces – men who never pleaded with time, never fled a mirror in shame or rage, but remained present to themselves

so glad to be themselves

Dear Yusuf,

A man of my acquaintance says your name to me every chance he gets. Feigns nonchalance, digresses in narrowing circles. Your consonants and vowels remain innocent in his mouth, even in the court of his harsh self-judgment. Late adopters, wanting to believe against all evidence that if soulmates exist we would meet ours *organically*, we would thrive in some imagined antiquity, early or late. He knows my skull houses a rare listening post for everyone who wishes to say your name, to realize their love for you one controlled burn at a time. Such feeling endures past all impediments, even your blithe inattention. Dear Yusuf! Such saints claim nothing for themselves. Devotees will bring heaps of marigolds and roses to their future shrines

Dear Yusuf,

Other poets can't accept my loss of you. They insist the end could not have been the end, they write me fervent new beginnings, they foreground charming and elaborate rationales for my benefit of the doubt. They sigh over my eyes and lustrous hair, swearing they were destined for you, that to have you behind the drawn curtain the God of Muslim modesty decreed is my prerogative, I would first have to lose the world

Dear Yusuf,

This is no era for reading dreams as portents. The self-proclaimed kings of today demand only quantifiable targets to hoard their feast against our famine, calculations to hide the wild sweat of the gambler at the card table, whose price of admission is empire

Dear Yusuf,

Storytellers of our patriarchs project eros onto the *absence of woman's will* far more ardently than onto feminine faces and bodies. They say that even I – who knew my own mind, who sought to act on what I wanted – I was captured helplessly while asleep, an inexperienced girl in thrall to a recurring dream, Jami's most beguiling explanation of how I was inspired or tricked into leaving home for Egypt, insisting that I must become the vizier's wife, and how he could not, or would not, and in the event *did not know me* –

According to the rules of wish fulfillment, audiences could only accept my exile with the reward of our union, which required the miracle of my regained youth, which in turn demanded the coy charms of a hymen that remained intact throughout every misadventure between my girlhood dreams of you and the widowhood that sent me into khalwa, whitening my hair and bending my spine

Dear Yusuf,

Love can end or elude the lover, but women's bodies don't have to go dry from endless yearning, transform into storied hag or feared daan. There are other abundances now: cheerful women doctors, prescription drugs, forest bathing, kitchen staff who, when I stop by for green curry with eggplant after swimming on Tuesday nights, scrawl hearts and smiley faces next to my name on the receipt. A farmer at my local market knows I like the early strawberries, and random strangers say that when their emotional-support dogs come to me for head pats it means they can tell I'm good people. Ladies of the city instruct their cooks to keep the fruit knives locked up, and never invite me to *their* banquets, and lavish approval on anything I do that seems difficult, or eccentric, or bold, as long as I do it alone, posting photos to prove it, with adequate self-deprecation

Zulaykha Addresses the Patriarchs

I pity the elders whose piety calls me anathema. Their faith must be vinegar whose mouths daily pucker with blame. They grow sour on hearing women speak of living beauty, suspicious of that pleasure heart's expansion lets loose in the limbs

Yet they make such a point of my presence in the story! That God created beauty, radiant and magnetic, in a man – I'm the mechanism of their proof. Among the ones who say I was rendered helpless with longing, even the ones demanding I should be killed for trying to possess him, no matter their elisions and equivocations, no matter. The centuries slip past, and I prevail. I remain vital. I catch them giving wary looks to the poets coming back for my act of witness. They would not dare write me out

Which lineage to claim – I am sometimes at a loss –
but I wish for no plague on your houses, Abrahamic siblings

Sa'di made me a chic idol-worshipping urbanite
Cairo's Karaites had Joseph put me to death at the point of a sword
illustrators of Bible stories for children *still* dress me up like Cleopatra
Jami triumphed in my remorse, claiming me for lovers of sirat al mustaqeem –
Marianne von Willemer addressed songs to her lover in my name

I reap my longevity from you all

From souls that cry to God
this many-coloured coat was made
and in the different registers of their cries
some of you invent reasons to go to war

I wish for no plague on your houses, Abrahamic siblings
I belong to you all

My poet bros run the hazard of confusing sex with worship. Drawn to paths of eloquence they grow used to adoration. Coded as feminine we become practised in deference, smoothing the path of their days. Stories live after even the most common of them, princely enjoyments turning gradually to boredom, to contempt. Why did they keep no record of our carefully written manuscripts, of the place where we composed those nazms, of the year when our mothers gave birth to us? Why must I ask them, who shrug, who go wide-eyed at my temerity, who stare around at each other for support, when I want to know who gave me my name? For our love's hovering constancy, its seeming surfeit, its fidelity that asks nothing for itself, leaving us wide open – to which they sing praises – to abandonment. I told myself I'd find a name unheard of among the chatter in bright halls, I'd look for a face lined by forbearance, keeping its grace hidden, keeping warm the hearth of inner life like a brown-feathered bird. I told myself I'd find love quietly

And men love Yusuf, gloating that no woman can have the man chosen by God for such extraordinary trials. Men love the noise and dust of building as much as the hushed places of worship they build, the serenity of walking unimpeded through the front doors. Men do not look for God in the solidarity lessons to be learned from garment-factory workers, or in the folded towels fresh from their mothers' laundry. They ignore the orange light indicating that the dust bag in the vacuum cleaner their brother-in-law gave them for a wedding present is full. When a woman speaks to them in lucid sentences, with the expectation of being heard, it comes to them as a disagreeable shock, *every time.* They make their lives smaller every time they refuse to imagine how the speed of my pulse, quickened by the sight of Yusuf, could beat at the base of their own throats

And no one thinks of Yusuf sighing, taking off his eyeglasses after a long day in the palace of the Pharaoh, ringing impatiently for the peon to bring him a glass of sweetened karkade, the career bureaucrat, accustomed to little perquisites, getting older. Even a mantle of honour has to be sent out for regular cleaning. Even the vizier born to prophetic lineage sometimes retires to the office sofa for a nap, a cushion between his knees, to relieve the twinge in his back

Ghalib Praises My Dream of Yusuf

EVEN NOW, THE PILLOW GIVES OFF A SCENT OF MUSK
 FROM HER HAIR
IN MY VISION, THE DREAM OF ZULAYKHA IS A REBUKE
 TO THE BEDDING

—MIRZA GHALIB

The second dream, the one Jami writes that I spent a year waiting for, when Yusuf promises to be mine *if I wait for him*, spelling out sexual proscription with glittering Persianate clarity, forbidding teeth from biting sugar, diamonds from piercing pearls – then disappears – I swoon – I tear my hair – my father fears for my sanity – I threaten to run away – my attendants chain me by the ankle –

What could have inspired Ghalib to write six couplets ending with the insomniac refrain – "of the bedding"? It's tempting to imagine Urdu's most celebrated poet searching vainly for a cool side to his pillow on a humid Delhi night, but we must take the literary high road. Only dilettantes would try to read a lover's fantasy, the lingering scent of the beloved's curls, as literal fact, or worse – as evidence. In the ghazal world, metre and metaphor, Yusuf-like, sternly rule out rapture of the flesh before poets compose a single line – so Ghalib makes a game of separation – sharpening melancholy with a hint of self-mockery –

From my intense longing for Yusuf, Jami tries to save me, weaving a fairy-tale epic, a lover innocently dreamed, a wish fulfilled, after bouts of madness and grief, dust and blood, self-harm threatened and actual, palaces and reed huts, rubies and pearls, brocade and silk, silver and gold – and an indulgent God – a magnanimous God –

Ghalib takes his cue from Jami's vision to praise my dreaming state above that of other hapless lovers, suggesting, perhaps, he and I are not so different. Whether the dream-object of desire mysteriously promises fidelity and disappears, or their very nonexistence drives the frenzied lover to imagine musk hanging in the air of their absence – Ghalib wrings enough humour from compassion to cover the cost of romantic human longing, reminding us why the form was invented –

if the beloved could be possessed, the ghazal could never be written

Zulaykha Surveys Her Art History

SUDDENLY IT SEEMED TO ME THAT THE ENTIRE WORLD WAS LIKE A PALACE WITH COUNTLESS ROOMS WHOSE DOORS OPENED INTO ONE ANOTHER. WE WERE ABLE TO PASS FROM ONE ROOM TO THE NEXT ONLY BY EXERCISING OUR MEMORIES AND IMAGINATIONS, BUT MOST OF US, IN OUR LAZINESS, RARELY EXERCISED THESE CAPACITIES, AND FOREVER REMAINED IN THE SAME ROOM.

—ORHAN PAMUK

Herat, 1488

If anguish keeps you listening too long
for coursers of destruction, drop inside a while

Inside is the place where you'll find
what it takes to remake the world

Kamal al Din brings forth the palace
he imagined I, Zulaykha, would commission

to prepare for the arrival of the paradise
he knew was coming for me

not the one in my head as I ran after Yusuf
but a variation one of my poets must have told him about –

paradise as event, not destination
reward manifest for the long patience

we all know I have yet to cultivate
painted only a handful of years

after Jami completed his epic
when no art could be replicated

except by replicating in extremis
the pains taken by the first artist

To the blaze of colour on the page
Kamal al Din applies nothing less

than the spirit of Herat, teaching novices
the art of slow looking, for which so many

declared they'd be honoured
to end their lives in blindness –

why must my painters take
their notions of honour so literally?

Palatial geometry at once lays open Behzad's world
and confines it – enchantment made miniature

exquisite surfeit secured
as if the master of the royal Persian atelier

hearing thunder reverberate
resolved to sneak the Pearl of Khorasan

past the next five hundred years of marauders
just to slake a future's parched imaginations –

shimmering, beckoning
blueprint for the repair of a world

Bukhara, circa 1525

In Bukhara's discerning eye I take my measure. Every scribe of Sa'di imagines desire brings me to my knees – but I love how we're composed. Every tactful apprentice marks out delicate frames and boxes to keep the poet's lines from overwhelming what the artist really wants.

Locked doors of lapis lazuli might yield to Yusuf in another second. Doors of jade open to twilight where laws of symmetry give way to enchantment – still, I love how we're composed. Our raised arms: a movement and a subtle echo, a rhyme and a faint refrain.

His bright face, unreliable narrator, turned towards mine. My fingers gripped insistent upon his wrist let slip the secret – the painter's on my side. For the next thousand years every woman will covet that green coat.

It could still happen. You never know.
That girl might win who refuses to let go.

Amsterdam, 1634

At the first glance my eyelids drop shut. I can't help it. My biggest influencers – those gaze-lowering Muslims, even the iconoclasts among them … to be seen anywhere east of the Atlantic with *this* Mrs. Potiphar would undo their patient and loving restorative work, redouble my scandal, bring it roaring back to life –

I look again, reluctantly. The artist gives out the story in his own vernacular – no fiery gold coronet, no halo marking heaven's favour, as if to say the sons of prophets may be found even in his own city; their labour-hewn bodies, their plaintive gestures, emit God's radiance too –

if only it weren't so hard on the eyes –

Joseph's revulsion, his hand throwing an omen of unforgiveness on the wife of Potiphar's sleeve, her torso condemned by the nightdress hitched above it – then the inviting softness Rembrandt gives the shadowed bed, that old idea, a friendly, hinting dark –

O Europe, *couldn't* you have stayed home in it –

Mrs. Potiphar's yearning more naked than her flesh, more palpable than the lines that barely suggest her face. As if secretly Rembrandt thinks he would have closed the drapes and comforted her –

As if, towards her, he only feels tenderness. Could anything ever make us admit – my ummah, my ahl-e-kitab, with all our scriptures so full of the word, how few of us can claim to know life under the gaze of such compassion –

Paris, 1876

Sensitive lithographer Auguste Racinet pays homage
to unknown artists of Hindustan who painted me first
Their work does not survive, so to stave off the sense of loss
I imagine them as children demanding their ayahs tell the story again
not sparing the simple frankness of the woman desiring
the beautiful man, not sparing how the women let slip
the sharp blades into soft palms and wrists so love of Yusuf
stings them too, with a citrus twist

Meticulous Auguste
marking leaf by dark green leaf into a slab of stone
until his tree of heaven covers the marble pavilion
his coral inlay echoed in our hair ornaments
his hand-knotted roses at our feet

Discreet fountain splashes and mists as if rehearsing
in whispers, my tearful remorse to come, *inna rabbi ghafooru rahim*

Auguste, did your century's Egyptomania leave you cold?
To all who now delight in your world, I'll play Indian princess forever
intricately adorned, stepping into a courtyard like a jewel box
where my ladies await their first sight
of a sun in his bright coronet, a sun in his green sleeves

Everyone still exults in the way I took care of it
when I said let's pare this matter down to the bone –
I've set out trays of oranges, sharpened the blades
making sure my guests want for nothing
I'm avid to see their mouths fall open
to hear astonishment clatter the knives

Kashmir Jannat Nazir, 1776

1

What if I never left home   what if I dreamed lucid
recalled where I belonged in time   made the dream take a different course
made Yusuf promise to come to me   awoke with mother-of-pearl
clasped in my fingers   his tilism of fidelity   like my vow to remain

from watermelons and pomegranates   pomegranates and watermelons
what if I remembered   I was eating light
what if catastrophe never struck   if a thousand years slipped past
like the Jhelum   faithful to its own haqq

then could I forget its name   could catastrophe strike
                my terrified subconscious
could a dream   become a trap   become a prison
could I really sink   into some man's dream of me   and believe it was mine

fed on pomegranates and watermelons   watermelons and pomegranates
could I leave   my home   whose name was –

2

Beauty flows past the young in the end. They obsess but never really take it in, they're on the way towards outsized ambitions, rightful entitlements. Beauty emanates from the young, surrounds and swirls past them, coming to rest

in the hollow at the base of throats gone spare, dry from long endurance, long absence, long self-abnegation

In the arrival of the self at its capacity for tenderness, beauty commands its fullest authority

Tender Kashmir, what richness, what subtle inflections wouldn't have flowed to me?

3

I let imagination arch my back. My hands clutch at knotted silk belonging. I'm guilty even now, with my mind on the brink of going to pieces. I ask the bleeding piece of earth to stay whole for me. I let imagination rest my arms as if cushioned by stories of flight narrated by the commander of winds himself

I've done nothing but hold myself in the shape of received forms, a kind of abeyance

If I'd been harder, less anxious to be liked, asked my mind to dream a different vessel, asked my two hands what world they could fashion – *no*

I sulked, my arms crossed, my presence becoming an absence where I might have decided brightly to see a prompt, endure a cold hour, arrive at steady breath, ask my two hands to take up their work, store a secret of persistence, fashion a container for worlds to come

What I cherished I held in suspense, never asking my two hands to stretch a canvas, stitch a conveyor, strike a match, weld and solder, press water from pulped fibre, attune myself in case of a melodic becoming

What is enough for a world? Will time let us hide in the green swaying curtain?

Convinced of absence, I fashion a subsistence, I precipitate a ghayr

Unknown painter, manuscripts are difficult. You knew *your* Zulaykha would have a turbulent future. That instinct for preservation – was it for your sake, or ours? Your skill is a shiraza – look at me, binding what's left of my world with *your* thread

The Ground of a Ghazal / Zamīn-e-Ghazal

And the life worth writing about, is it worth living alone, somewhere?
The resolute course no Kashmiran reverses, having flown somewhere

Why do we call it sublimity, that terrifying cosmic indifference?
Does it lessen mortal pain to carve a name in stone somewhere?

Another xenophobe bans another Muslim thing – but every 29th of January
Même les péquistes les plus haineux wear a public face to atone somewhere

I wish their rock faces would erode faster, those freedom-confounding fathers
Every time I hear another sister in dread of forced birth groan somewhere

Like summer solstice, Aleppo kept time by the sung poems of Andalucia
The white moon never rose over us but our time in exile shone somewhere

Our poetics of solidarity bloom, and a rose fills police with suspicion
They outlaw the metaphor but still can't kill the seed sown somewhere

The mystery of those pages left blank – so strange for a calligrapher! As if
to Yusuf and Zulaykha, Mirak yielded his own zamīn, his own *somewhere*

(*for Khashayar Mohammadi and Mudasir Gul*)

Zulaykha Considers Her Options

SAID YUSUF: TELL ME, ZULAYKHA, WHAT BECAME OF YOUR
YOUTH? ... YOUR SHINING BEAUTY?
SAID ZULAYKHA: I SACRIFICED THEM TO MY PASSION FOR YOU

—PUNJABI QAWWALI SUNG BY NUSRAT FATEH ALI KHAN

There's a game I play, with time, against time. You've heard of it. Desperation brings you to the stark face of the cliff. You got here by your own will – you'll have to make a choice, take the step that will open you to the unknown – but another part of you, soft, faltering, replays a promise of enchantment, lapsing into memory like an illness in childhood that stings even strict parents into moods of indulgence –

I lapse into a memory of Yusuf this way, unplanned encounter already becoming a dream, his face lit by late-afternoon gold, my sight going blank as if my disbelief could not hold his image steady

This would be the moment, memory suggests, you would go back to if you could, isn't it, when his eyes met yours, that light hovered above your head, that possibility flickered before polite convention broke your silence

Treacherous memory, shady swindler, yes, damn you, I want to be her again – over her clear eyes, the admiring makeup-counter staff had sighed, *they are your fortune* – her throat unlined, her hands supple, free of pain, and the moment, the possibility – were mine

But what if beauty only dwells in the tender apprehension of damage which hasn't happened yet?

Whatever the poet promised, whatever he owed his audience – whatever precipice we all come to, abandoned, left for dead in the dust off roads built by imperial armies –

Doesn't it bring us low, the wish to go back, the vain lust to relive a few vital hours, to reverse a life towards the pearls and emeralds of wish fulfillment?

For all that Jami triumphs in my remorse, claiming me for lovers of sirat al mustaqeem – later, he turns ambivalent, overheated, lurid –

It's true the patriarchs expect all widows to become irrational harridans, but I believed in beauty's creator, Yusuf's God. Why would I pluck out my own eyes?

And why would I give up the hard-won friendship with myself? Fall backward off time's sheer cliff with no belay? The fantasy betrays every azizatu nafsiha –

No – I won't be her again – that girl off her head in desire's first throes, convinced she has plumbed depths – attained summits worthy of mortals –

She has waded into mere shallows

Zulaykha Alone

YOU'RE WITHDRAWING FROM ME, YOU HOUR.
THE BEATING OF YOUR WINGS LEAVES ME BRUISED.
ALONE: WHAT SHALL I DO WITH MY MOUTH?
WITH MY NIGHT? WITH MY DAY?

—RAINER MARIA RILKE

What a miracle it is, to *wake up every day*. And still, how hard it is *to wake up and be good*. How hard it is to wake up and *still* be good, to be good *again*. How hard it is to wake up and face the necessity of *believing* in my own goodness again. To fumble around for it like a pair of spectacles I can't see without, fearful that this time it's lost, it's really gone. These are the mornings the bereft know, we who have been stripped of belonging, turfed out of worlds we loved. Such selves as remain to us in the aftermath of devastation, we regard with wariness. How hard it is not to think *what's to stop this self, too, from vanishing at any moment*? Philosophers shake their heads sadly at the locked door where I keep knocking. How hard it is not to argue, *but I was given such a dazzling welcome here once*. The mystics try to convince me that mirrors roam the universe in search of souls like mine to reflect.

How hard it is not to say, *I'm itching to throw stones.*

Voices of my time call me into their melodies. Voices to which I'd given half my attention in the past now hold me rapt, following every note, amazed by their subtle buildup to crescendos of glory. I marvel, I exult in their logic, assured I will overcome what presses me down, I will take flight into rosy dawns. They offer transcendence as exhortative as any chorus in Arabic or Greek, Latin or Punjabi, promising we will arrive at stations of radiant certainty.

I fear it before I can learn to trust it. That solitude lets my thoughts form and spread like foliage in sunlight.

Retrospect is not the domain of melancholy alone.

Delight lurks there too.

I let myself remember the first time I saw Yusuf.

My disbelief, as if I'd split in two, in what my eyes could convey to my brain. That a man could give such pleasure merely by possessing a face! I laugh now, remembering my shock on receiving such communication from God or the universe I'd only begged for a little dignity, just a little peace of mind. Pleasure demanding its right of way over all my senses before modesty intervened with its usual threats and promises.

[Dear God, why did You make Yusuf?
Was he Your gauntlet, flung down into the well
and You, The Jealous, daring us
not to make him Your rival?
Yours, Zulaykha]

The song makes its home in those parts of my consciousness formed in immersive belonging now vanished, the parts that most crave beginning, middle, and enveloping, victorious end. Music comes back to me in a summer when much of the known world has fled, its familiar rhythms have fallen silent, my body is freed of those narrow confines where to be seen is to be censured. The symphony of voices has waited all this time to fill my house of being, to reveal its dimensions of sound, how much light it can hold – I want to run, to fly, along the course they have charted for me – to course like a river in love with their idea.

Does the Earth form our human selves with its round fullness, its acts of life giving, or is the Earth formed in answer to the eyes of its lovers? How much it means to have a face to turn to the world, to walk out in it reflecting everything we might look upon with unhurried calm, without fear, moving always and only towards whatever instructs by delight; as if to search only for that mirror.

For a golden summer a kind of stasis holds an entire world in thrall. Isolation becomes a general virtue, a civic duty. We wave to each other on screens, shagirds wax lyrical, now at a verse of Sa'di, now at a verse of Hafez, we make gestures of warm embrace. Fall returns us to sinister light, filtered by a thick pall of smoke, general anxiety. I glimpse eight of my neighbours dancing in pairs with cool grace, as if their inherited rhythms could dispell the effects of burning –

The world slips off its unaccustomed garment of collective duty – people who know love take shelter in love's accepted tokens and enduring solemnities – others whisper in other tongues that the world or some authorized reports of it will endure, but that it must change –

The world could not be the same again, the world I thought the singers of my time were promising I could reach. The song that had called me to follow its melody was itself the world, the singer's gladness in its refrain was its reward. I could admire, rehearse, remember – and then I would have to produce my own sound.

If worship dwells in gratitude, benediction comes from mirrors and faces which cannot lie. I fed upon beauty, I shrank from ugliness. I wanted only that exaltation which could expand and enrich and revive and heal and retrieve what I was always at risk of losing. To wear the face of a continuing self, to see your skin's fidelity to its bones and sinews begin to slacken – must this mean fidelity releases its hold on hope, its belief in love's reward and blessing? To meet in your mirror the new pain in the question, *this face, what was it for?*

Days when I feel drawn to metaphor of needle and thread. Why do pen and ink release their primary hold? The question never tests my patience as sorely as the task the turbulent decades have left me, their demand of diligent repair. Perhaps it's that I choose not to look at the entire cloudy mess but just what my hands can hold: the faintly creamy hue of the page, sharp point of the pen that appears some days less to write than to stitch the words I was compelled to pick apart the week before in clearer lines –

I’m glad to follow poets who went searching in this direction before me – artists who made the mirrors where I most wish to behold my self, where I can live in the service of wholeness, its imagining and creation. It will be the task of those to come after me to say whether I supported their steadfastness enough to change the world we still have time to name together –

And when we learned to name the precise forms of violence wrought by the lies of the powerful over us, whether our act of naming proved their undoing.

I'm only pulled away from this patient stitching, these acts of repair,
at every moment the machines command my attention,
frontier of sentience I'm constantly forgetting and relearning to defend

Say that tyrants tore away so many possible worlds from us
that the face of one man became a powerful reminder in this one –

Say the lines of his beauty mirrored the harmony
of the world I was shocked to remember I carried within

Say a world ruled by love of harmony
is what I pulled him towards
when I pulled him towards me

Not all environments built for solace take three-dimensional form. Someone wrote a song, someone left safe passage, for your voice to feel its way through the dark, like red hand marks left by painters thirty-six thousand years ago in the Chauvet Caves. High notes and low notes and rests that say, *here is where Ms. Lauryn Hill, with only her breath, makes you feel as if her pain is going to claw its way out of your own chest*, or *from this depth, Chris Cornell fearlessly scaled those heights*, or *here is where Bootstraps excavates the lonely path Whitney Houston walked when no one else could hear it*, and *listen, Bulleh Shah saved compassion's blaze for you in the throat of Punjab, answering life with life.*

I lived through this day. I will probably forget it, pearl slipping off a chain. Hours that leave no discernible trace. I carried dead roses down the stairs and paused at the lip of the compost bin. Their pinks intensified when the water of life left them, almost glowing under the grey February clouds. Their lives were their own, irreducible to human greed or other vanities we give the guise of love. I lived through this day and I will probably forget it, small miracle of hours leaving no anguish, like an unanticipated message from a friend that never reaches me; like waking to sunlight shining on my hands.

Ashura

SHE TOOK A STONE, AND LIKE ABRAHAM, SHATTERED THE IDOL WITH IT.

—HAKIM NURUDDIN ABDURRAHMAN JAMI

Apology for anachronism I'll make none. I honour the witnesses who reach past the centuries to retrieve imprints of the disappeared: melodies, rooms, horses. Moments defined by a perfume, carried in a muezzin's voice. The absence my death will create wears a groove in someone else's memory – that's how the thought walks with me. *Companion, I did not summon you.*

Other women are afraid to ask how I survive the days. I walk east when I want out of their loop, seeking firs for their gloaming, formidable, eating all the ambient light, hinting at spirits, guardian beings I have no wish to importune. I sidle past their inviting dark, shyly wishing I knew their language, to say a graceful hello. How many of my selves have walked the monotony of this road? I'm furthest from that one who was brave because she didn't know another way to be. I'm sore-eyed from transformations worked on land as on women's bodies, dismantlings, uprootings, diggings, pavings. Young and anxious, young and happy, anxious again and still young, older and anxious, older and alone. Even here, I think, I was most myself when walking, eager, intent on arrival and its pleasures. I'm a body swathed in successions of grey sweaters, stammerings, fluencies, breakages, refusals, obediences, boots skimming the distance to the nearest exit, echoes of cruelties, no longer secret, for which I will no longer lack language. Other women are afraid to ask how I survive the days.

Things I'll leave behind when I die rise to mind when I walk. I slid that ring on my finger to dwell a while in the space between my raw self and the geologic perfection of the shining object, void of all purpose or striving. I picked up self-adornment much later in life than these arts of reading and writing. Is it a kind of amnesia that makes me never tire of looking, of trying new forms? Even regarding those objects I buy to prolong my pleasure in the present, mortality moves assiduously into my consciousness. Who will rifle among the objects I looked at, paid for, wore? I can never encompass as much of language as I want, never conduct enough meaning to draw people closer together across the chasms I inherited at birth. If I could somehow be buried in language, if my body could break down into components of words and letters, would that reconcile me to death's disassemblage?

Would I meet with other souls in an afterlife saray? Would watching mortals make sense of us, cope with the outcomes of our choices, bring relief? I always coveted omniscience. But I speak of coveting as one alive, therefore limited, defaulting too often to the shape of solitude without its presence, holding myself not to hopes of happiness but detachment, disinterest, a wish to marvel at the narrative implausibility of the other humans, and – dearly – to remain free of mine. The religions urge us to aspire to varying images of paradise, the mystics – after my own heart, sometimes – want divine union, to dissolve into infinite light. I know the fulfillment of their longing would bring the end of language, our most enduring home on this earth, our most tensile means of surviving ikhtilaf, whereby our acts of naming become holy.

Does longing for mystical union constitute a desire for a silent realm? Where all is oneness, can there be any need to speak? To parse feelings and facts, warnings and intentions, into verbs and adjectives and nouns – was this not the first work of the first survivors of fires, blizzards, predators, childbirth? Conditions evoking awe, immanence, the desire to seal an earthquake or an angel bearing prophecy into collective memory, to mark time ever afterwards by what shook their bones. Every syllable a stone towards a bridge where meaning passes from stranger to wary stranger until the story encircles them both. As for stones in rings and earrings, I'll leave them all behind as ciphers for memory, mute pebbles to be dashed against so many other piles of time.

Akhlaq

CAT-CLAW AT THE MOUSE'S BACK, SHE
TEARS HIS SHIRT IN HER WANTING –
THEN LIES TO PROTECT HERSELF.

OH, HOW HE WISHES HE COULD THROW DOWN A MANTLE
OF HONOUR OVER HER.

—DOYALI ISLAM

pulled as if by powerful updraft
into the realm of ecstasy

senses pervading soul
soul enveloping senses

it was the high point of his existence
when I looked at him

spontaneous utterance
of pure conscience

to reach for the hem of the garment
whether with love or desire

mattered nothing –
the reaching was all

Inheritance

Daughters I'll never have, the house of our patriarchs casts a much longer shadow over the earth than I realized. After I left its walls, this became my work: measuring the extent of its reach, puzzling over why the sun never set over its roof.

Daughters I'll never have, do not let patriarchs importune you too early with stories of strong women who stifled their thirst through the day and spilled their cup of water at night, who pushed through illness and fatigue to warn others of the coming plague, who sacrificed their portion of the weekly meat for a brother, who kept silent in the face of vulgar chatter and harsh pronouncements, who spoke from behind a partition or who spoke not at all, who led fierce battles on horseback only to cry aloud in regret – a wish to be forgotten, a wish to be dust.

Daughters I'll never have, I've either thrown off or been turfed out of the confines of whatever's possible in a life like mine, a human being overdetermined as woman, as sign of anathema. I held to this illuminated page for ballast, this space where I was imagined, sung, venerated, given a name – or I will be, depending on where in time you light up the rooms of your births –

I was not always grateful for the wilderness in which this freedom came to be mine –

Daughters I'll never have, you who come into the world with a genius for transmuting love into attention, anticipating the needs of others before they utter the word, becoming little mothers before you've been children, who ask of others, "*What are you going through?*" before you spare a thought for yourselves, do not become overawed by the sacrifices and self-denials of women whose names the patriarchs only safeguarded for your stern instruction. Revere those names whose auras remain strong, but do not take up their burdens. Live in the present, which offers you its gifts, and where you have the right to be.

Zulaykha Is Floored by Emily Dickinson's Poem 1311

ART THOU THE THING I WANTED?
BEGONE – MY TOOTH HAS GROWN –

—EMILY DICKINSON

Time curdles, harsh medicine, in the back of my throat. The jolt of her past tense, the severity of her retrospect – but I want to keep faith with her art. Not guess at how many degrees separate the acute brevity of the line from what hunger breathed in the living poet, even when I want to rebel, claim as mine a fidelity over which time has no power

As if daring us not to imagine the courage overtaking the hunger
        its infinitely lonelier growth
As if the short bursts of her words barely escaped her greater
        implacable silence

Her proud renunciation inspires awe. Can such resolve come from a mind at peace? Waves of humans recede from shores of friendship with shrugs of helplessness, praising the strength of the one they're leaving. My answering propensity for self-denial, like the return to a birthplace, as forced as any bid for social approval, as if Ramadan were the factory setting for the human temperament. I want to rebel. My skin craves simple delight, the warmth of hands, the luxury of serene continuity, the fidelity to which my longing keeps turning, let other poets call it an addiction, a delusion

Hallāj, meet Emily
Emily, meet Hallāj

Emily Dickinson's Work Ethic

Everyone finds their own way to poetry
How many have come to it, how many are still to come
trailing skirts through warm summer dust
carrying yellow balloons, garlic and onions
rain-spotted photos of ancestors
writing children's jam-stained faces
into a sonnet with a distracted air
confiding to friends that yes, I do work best alone
but without the cup you poured for me that morning
I would have lost the thread, the page where I read that poem
that sparked my memory of the word, let me seize it
wipe the tarnish of two centuries from its filigree

Poetry might flood the senses like the cool relief
of leaning into an open freezer at the corner store
in search of a banana popsicle on a hot day in July

It could arrive at midnight, in the scrape of tall weeds
swept along the car doors while you're lost on a dirt road
on the day your cousin got their license to drive

It might exhilarate like a lurch in the stomach
of someone in a cold grey corporate tower elevator
after teaching suits at a performance review
precisely how to say their musical name
securing a raise

It could astonish someone with constricted breath at a closed window
with the sight of salsa dancers in the alley below, turning and swaying
to inaudible music in the smoke-filled air of a September afternoon
setting forever after a standard for elegance and surprise –
that life on this earth is meant for dancing, not burning

Everyone finds their own way to poetry

Not many would adopt Emily's ferociously guarded hours
but there are days when I hear my lineage of mystics
their passionate disavowals
echoed in the way she closed her doors
to everything except diligent exactitude
and compressed fluency, the lyric opening
just enough for a shimmer of uncertainty to arise
even from the perfection of the word

we covet like a gem

Introspective Ghazal

To girls guarded as girls, must love prove probity of sex?
To boys willed to be boys, must love belie vanity of sex?

So much now depends on being always, everywhere *seen*
Pure cinema – didn't early critics so praise subtlety of sex?

Zulaykha only smiles when posing rivals clutch Yusuf's arm
His distracted face in blue phone-glow, though – there's the sting –
the ever-present interruptibility of sex

No gossip stokes scandal like a supreme court misogynist
To corrode, to its very heart, the incorruptibility of sex

Could what passed between them be called a mere glance
if ex post facto legal jargon hid its a priori guarantee of sex?

I honour the poets and painters in whose mystic hearts
Zulaykha's fidelity persists, exalting a spirituality of sex

Won't Rahat bring this bakvaas to some decorous end?
Or will she persist in madness – to look for dignity in sex?

Shukrana

The global lineage of Zulaykha can be traced back for nearly a thousand years and even beyond that to pre-Islamic, Persian, and Hellenic roots, thanks to meticulous research and spirited translation work by historians and literary critics spending the best years of their lives deep in the scriptural, poetic, musical, artistic, and folk literary sources. Scholars Marc S. Bernstein, Marina Warner, Claire Jacobsen, and Jami's intrepid English-language translator David Pendlebury affirm the interdependence of early Islamic, Jewish, and Christian prophetic stories as collective memory, shared inheritance. Their work kept me reassuring company as I wrote *The Book of Z.*

I am inexpressibly grateful to Tina Rahimi, my Persian poetry teacher, and to Professor Frances Pritchett, creator and guardian of the legendary online archive of the Divan-e Ghalib, among other treasures of Urdu literature dear to the hearts of the ahl-e-zubaan. "If Ghalib wants you," she counsels, "against all odds he will reach out and grab you; he chooses his own readers ..."

To Simone Weil, author of the question, "What are you going through?"

To Marguerite Pigeon and Fatima ElKalay, peerless first readers. To Mohja Kahf for pointing me toward the enigma of the Isra'iliyyat, and Khashayar Mohammadi for commending my path as khalwa. To Cross Li for their insightful comments. To my son Aijaz for his kindness and ethics of care.

To my mentor A.E. Stallings and my cohort of writers at the wonderful 2024 Summer Writers Residency, and to the staff at the Banff Centre for the Arts, for their love of what they do. I'm grateful to Professor Mo Pareles for inviting me to share the world of Zulaykha with their students and colleagues in the English Department at UBC. Shukriya to Umair Parvez and Sarah Khan for supplying colloquial and musical Zulaykha citations that still haunt our cultural ether.

For a long time I kept *Z* to myself, until Catriona Strang asked what else I was working on, and without hesitation said, "You have to do this." I'm extremely thankful to her and to the enduring presence, commitment, and care of everyone at Talonbooks on this literary landscape.

Support from the Canada Council for the Arts allowed me to keep the wolves from the door through another heartless winter. Alhamdulillah. What a privilege.

Art Works Referred to in "Zulaykha Surveys Her Art History"

All art works cited are in the public domain and searchable online. "Herat, 1488" refers to *The Seduction of Yusuf* by Kamal al-Din Behzad, folio from the *Būstan* (orchard) of Sa'di, the thirteenth century Persian poet, painted in Herat in 1488 (then in Khorasan, now in modern-day Afghanistan), Egyptian National Library and Archives, Cairo.

"Bukhara, circa 1525" refers to *Yusuf and Zulaikha,* ink, opaque watercolour, and gold on paper, artist unknown. Folio from an edition of the *Būstan* (orchard) of Sa'di. This painted or illuminated poetry manuscript, made in Bukhara circa 1525–1535, during the more than two hundred years of Safavid reign over the Persian empire, is on display at the Metropolitan Museum of Art in New York.

"Amsterdam, 1634" refers to *Joseph and Potiphar's Wife,* 1634, etching by Rembrandt van Rijn, Amsterdam, privately held.

"Paris, 1876" refers to a lithographic print by Auguste Racinet, from the section "Inde/India" in *Le Costume Historique* (The Complete Costume History), published in Paris in six volumes between 1876 and 1888. In the style of a Mughal miniature painting, the image depicts Yusuf being brought out by Zulaykha in the midst of walled garden, with a marble pavilion, carpets, a fountain, flowerbeds, and foliage. A group of women seated in the foreground, holding oranges and fruit knives, have unwittingly pierced their own hands instead, where trickles of blood are clearly visible. All of the figures are resplendently dressed in lavish gold fabrics and jewelry.

"Kashmir Jannat Nazir, 1776" and "The Ground of a Ghazal/Zamin-e-Ghazal" are inspired by a volume of Jāmi's *Yusuf and Zulaikha* which contains thirty-four minature paintings of scenes from the epic. The book's colophon identifies the calligrapher as Muhammad Mirak, and "Kashmir, the little paradise, 1776" as the place and date where it was commissioned and bound. The volume is held in the Rare Books Collection at the Walters Art Museum in Baltimore.

Epigraph Sources

Dickinson, Emily. Poem 1311, "Art thou the thing I wanted?" In *Dickinson: Selected Poems and Commentaries*, edited with commentary by Helen Vendler. The Belknap Press, 2010.

Donne, John. "To His Mistress Going to Bed." *Poetry Foundation*. poetryfoundation.org/poems/50340/to-his-mistress-going-to-bed.

Ghalib, Mirza. "Ghazal 194." [1816]. *A Desertful of Roses: The Divan-e Ghalib* (website). franpritchett.com/00ghalib/194/index_194.html. Translated by Rahat Kurd.

Islam, Doyali Farah. "captive." *Yūsuf and the Lotus Flower*. Buschek Books, 2011.

Jami, Hakim Nuruddin Abdurrahman. *Yusuf and Zulaikha: An Allegorical Romance*. Edited and translated by David Pendlebury. The Octagon Press, 1980.

Pamuk, Orhan. *My Name Is Red*. Translated by Erdağ M. Göknar. Alfred A. Knopf, 2001.

Khan, Nusrat Fateh Ali, vocalist. "Qissa Yusaf Alahislam," from the album *Yusuf Zulaikha, Ustad Nusrat Fateh Ali Khan*, vol. 98. Star Compact Disc CDSR 2271, 1993. Lyrics unattributed. Translated by Rahat Kurd.

Rilke, Rainer Maria. "The Poet." *New Poems [1907]*. Translated by Edward Snow. North Point Press, 1984.

Sells, Michael. *Stations of Desire: Love Elegies from Ibn 'Arabi and New Poems*. Ibis Editions, 2000.

Rahat Kurd dwells on the ancestral zamīn of the xʷməθkʷəy̓m (Musqueam), Sḵwx̱wú7mesh (Squamish), and səlilwətaɬ (Tsleil-Waututh) Nations and dreams of being a papermaker and calligrapher in eighteenth-century Kashmir.